Lights, Symbols And Angels!

Six Worship Resources For Advent/Christmas

Cynthia E. Cowen

CSS Publishing Company, Inc., Lima, Ohio

LIGHTS, SYMBOLS AND ANGELS!

Copyright © 1999 by
CSS Publishing Company, Inc.
Lima, Ohio

The original purchaser may photocopy material in this publication for use as it was in-
tended (i.e., worship material for worship use; educational material for classroom use;
dramatic material for staging or production). No additional permission is required from
the publisher for such copying by the original purchaser only. Inquiries should be ad-
dressed to: Permissions, CSS Publishing Company, Inc., P.O. Box 4503, Lima, Ohio 45802-
4503.

Some scripture quotations are from the *New Revised Standard Version of the Bible*, copyright 1989 by the Division of Christian Education of the National Council of the Churches
of Christ in the USA. Used by permission.

Some scripture quotations are from the *Holy Bible, New International Version*. Copyright
© 1973, 1978, 1984 International Bible Society. Used by permission of Zondervan Bible
Publishers. All rights reserved.

Library of Congress Cataloging-in-Publication Data

Cowen, Cynthia E., 1947-
   Lights, symbols, and angels : six worship resources for Advent, Christmas / Cynthia
Cowen.
      p.   cm.
   ISBN 0-7880-1517-6 (pbk. : alk. paper)
   1. Advent. 2. Christmas. 3. Worship programs. I. Title.
BV40.M63   1999
263'.91—dc21   99-37622
                                                                                  CIP

ISBN: 0-7880-1517-6   PRINTED IN U.S.A.

I would like to dedicate this resource to those who inspired me to create it: my senior high youth at Our Saviour's, who are always game to doing skits which are fun and inspiring, and my Women of the ELCA Circle of Joy, who worked hard at creating a whole weekend teaching on the ministry of angels — especially my musical friend, Sally Karttunen. I am encouraged and affirmed as a writer by both youth and women. What a joy it is to create resources for them, to watch them begin to create on their own, to grow in their confidence as worship leaders, and to see God's Holy Spirit work through all of us to draw people closer to our Lord.

Lights, Symbols And Angels!

This Advent/Christmas resource is designed to help a busy pastor, Sunday school coordinator, youth director, minister of music, youth group, Christian education director, or head of women's ministry. This book contains six resources which may be used during this prime time in the life of the church.

Lights

Symbols

An ideal resource for a fellowship potluck, a women's tea or program, a mid-week worship service, or an intergenerational event. This program combines the meaning behind Christmas symbols and uses a variety of Christmas carols.

Angels

Is your youth group in charge of a mid-week service? Well, let those *angels* take part in this service designed for as many participants as you have. Litanies designed around angels focus the worshiper on God's angelic hosts. A skit, "Hark! It's Harold And The Angel Band," uses Gabe (the archangel Gabriel disguised as a stock boy) and Mr. Grumpy and Mr. Grumpier (old men shopping at Heaven's Grocery Store who encounter each other) and an Angel Band led by Harold. Unique songs help to drive home the point that God is creating Christmas in our midst once again.

This resource can be used as a Sunday worship experience, a mid-week service, or a special Advent program. The worship is designed around the theme of angels. Select four witnesses who can share a story of an angel, in the flesh or heavenly, in their lives. A baseball theme is used with appropriate hymns using angels.

A Christmas Celebration

Wind up your Advent journey with this order of worship for Christmas Eve. "A Christmas Celebration" celebrates Jesus' birth through readings, litanies, and Christmas music. The celebration of Holy Communion and the singing of "Silent Night" by candlelight help to make this service a meaningful one for all involved.

Lights

O COME, BLESSED LIGHT OF THE WORLD!

Advent Greetings From The Light Of The World!

Simeon, a righteous and devout man, was looking forward to the consolation of Israel. He just happened to be in the Temple the day Mary and Joseph brought the baby Jesus there. When the old man's eyes fell upon the infant, the Holy Spirit prompted him to take the baby and praise God, saying, "Master, now you are dismissing your servant in peace, according to your word; for my eyes have seen your salvation, which you have prepared in the presence of all peoples, a *light* for revelation to the Gentiles and for glory to your people Israel" (Luke 2:29-32).

Light — the opposite of darkness; *light* — a mental or spiritual illumination or enlightenment; *light* — that which furnishes, or is the source of, light, such as the sun, a star, candle, lamp, and so on. These are but three definitions for "light" as found in Webster's dictionary. All three point to a focus for us in our Advent preparation. Our Advent prayer then will be: "O Come, Blessed Light of the World!"

As we begin our preparations for Christmas, many of us will drag out the tree lights to see if bulbs need to be replaced. A string of lights with bad bulbs will leave our tree in darkness. Yet a string of lights with good bulbs is of no use if not plugged in. Advent is that time to plug in once again to the *light* which has been revealed to the world in the birth of the Christ Child. Our Advent journey enables Christians to gain spiritual enlightenment as we recall how much God loves us and how he chose to send Jesus to redeem us. The light which Simeon saw and which we see today in the Holy Infant furnishes each one of us with a source of light that can never grow dim or go out. Our red and green candles may burn down this Christmas season. Our tree lights may burn out. But Jesus, the source of *true light*, can never be extinguished.

As you daily follow the Advent Wreath Lighting Ceremony, *O Come, Blessed Light of the World!* and Advent suggestions which

11

use **The Light Of The Advent Candle, The Light Of The Word,** and **the Light Of Action**, your Advent journey will be enhanced. It is our prayer that you will use this Advent resource as an opportunity to return to the Lord with all your heart. Take time each day to reflect on the message of light as you read the Word, consider the reflections, pray the prayers which will help you recall the many ways God comes as the light and calls you to be a "light" to the world, and then respond in your actions. As Jesus reflected the light of God's love, we are called to shine forth with that same love. Add your light to ours as we let our lights shine to the glory of God! Have a blessed Advent journey.

Introduction

The one who testifies to these things says, "Surely I am coming soon." Amen. Come, Lord Jesus!
— Revelation 22:20

Advent is the time once again to prepare the heart to receive the Blessed Light of the World, Jesus our Lord and our Savior. During the season of Advent we hear the voice of one crying in the wilderness, "Prepare the way of the Lord, make his paths straight" (Matthew 3:3). Therefore, Advent challenges us to examine our hearts as God's light reveals our sin and God's grace brings forgiveness and reveals his love.

John the Baptist came preaching repentance, a turning from sin. Those who live in the darkness are called to embrace the light of their salvation, Jesus the Christ. "John came as a witness to testify to the light, so that all might believe through him. He himself was not the light, but he came to testify to the light. The true light, which enlightens everyone, was coming into the world" (John 1:7-9).

As you journey, using your Advent Wreath and devotional materials, let the light of our Lord shine upon your heart. Allow the Lord to turn you into his light that you may shine forth as a beacon of hope to others. May your Advent journey be blessed with an ever-increasing illumination of the Child of Bethlehem as you begin your journey by praying, "O come, Blessed Light of the World!"

Advent Wreath Cerermony

First Week Of Advent

The Light Of The Advent Candle: As you light the first Advent candle, the "Prophecy Candle," recall the prophet Isaiah's words, "The people who walked in darkness have seen a great light; those who lived in a land of deep darkness — on them light has shined" (Isaiah 9:2).

The Light Of The Word: After lighting the first candle in your Advent wreath, read the scripture passage assigned for that day for enlightenment. God still speaks to his people today.

Readings For The First Week Of Advent

Sunday: Genesis 1:1-4
Key Verse: "Then God said, 'Let there be light'; and there was light" (Genesis 1:3).
Reflection

"Mommy, Mommy!" a child cries out from the darkness of her room. Her mother rushes in and flicks on the light. The child holds out her arms to be comforted.

Light breaks into darkness and makes us feel safe. Consider how the light of God's love can make us feel secure in the face of those things which frighten us. Share about a time when you found comfort from God in the face of a frightening situation.
Prayer

Lord God, dispel the darkness which seeks to engulf me. Speak and show me the goodness of your light. Amen.

Monday: Isaiah 9:2-7

Key Verse: "The people who walked in darkness have seen a great light; those who lived in a land of deep darkness — on them the light has shined" (Isaiah 9:2).

Reflection

"Who goes there?" the young boy cried out from inside his backyard tent. As he watched an approaching figure coming toward him through the night, he noticed how the bright beam of a flashlight illuminated the path before the intruder.

"It's just me, son, coming to check if you and your friends need anything before I go to sleep for the night," his father's voice replied.

"No, but thanks for asking."

The father returned to the house at peace knowing his son and friends were secure for the night.

Jesus, the Prince of Peace, is the light which shines into our darkened souls to bring salvation. The Father sent the Son because he loved us and wanted to restore us to a right relationship with him. Know that there is no darkness so deep that the Father's light and love cannot enter.

Prayer

Lord God, thank you for sending Jesus to be our Savior. I turn from the darkness and embrace the light. Amen.

Tuesday: Isaiah 42:5-9

Key Verse: "I am the Lord, I have called you in righteousness, I have taken you by the hand and kept you; I have given you as a covenant to the people, a light to the nations" (Isaiah 42:6).

Reflection

Along the coast lighthouses stand as silent sentinels during the day. At night their bright beams shine forth as beacons to ships at sea.

God has selected you to be lights to those who do not yet know Jesus. Shine with the love of Christ as you help others to find their way to the knowledge of the one who is the True Light.

Prayer

Lord God, take me by the hand and lead me through this life. Help me to shine brightly with the light of your love. Amen.

Wednesday: Isaiah 60:1-3
Key Verse: "Arise, shine; for your light has come, and the glory of the Lord has risen upon you" (Isaiah 60:1).
Reflection
"Time to get up," Grandma called as she threw up the shade. The morning light flooded the room and announced that a new day had dawned in the world.

Isaiah tells us that all nations will come to the light of recognition of God's glory. We find that glory revealed in Christ. As we eagerly embrace each new day, we will find that God's light is shining upon us. Let that light be over you this week.
Prayer
Lord God, I rejoice in the light of each new day. Help me to live each moment to your glory. Amen.

Thursday: John 1:1-5
Key Verse: "The light shines in the darkness, and the darkness did not overcome it" (John 1:5).
Reflection
Outside a lamppost stood silhouetted in the darkness. Its glass dome began to be covered with falling snow. It was a bad night to be outside. Suddenly someone threw an inside switch on, and light shone out to welcome family or stranger home.

Jesus is that light which the darkness cannot overcome. He is the one who welcomes all people home. No one is a stranger to God. He receives all who come to him and makes them a part of the family through Christ.
Prayer
Lord God, you created all things through Jesus. Let his light shine in me, creating new life and flooding my soul with peace. Amen.

Friday: John 1:6-9
Key Verse: "He came as a witness to testify to the light, so that all might believe through him" (John 1:7).

Reflection

"Do you swear that the testimony you are about to give is true?" a court clerk asked the witness as she was sworn in.

"I do," came a confident reply.

John the Baptist was not the Messiah, God's Anointed. He was one who confidently pointed to the light of God's truth as it had been shown to him. John came to testify that God had sent a Savior into the world. His testimony and ours bear witness to Christ's presence in the world. Share a time when you have witnessed to your faith in Jesus. Was it difficult?

Prayer

Lord God, forgive me when I fail to share with others how much you mean to me. Help me to be more comfortable in witnessing to those around me. Amen.

Saturday: John 8:12

Key Verse: "Again Jesus spoke to them, saying, 'I am the light of the world. Whoever follows me will never walk in darkness but will have the light of life' " (John 8:12).

Reflection

The sky was speckled with what appeared to be a thousand tiny lights. The Milky Way was spectacular as astronomy students used their telescopes to get a better view of the heavenly objects.

Natural wonders in the sky awe and amaze us. Yet Jesus tells us that he is the light of the world. He is the one who shines so brightly that as we follow him we will be overwhelmed by all that he has to show us. Talk about how God works in nature to reveal himself to us.

Prayer

Lord God, help me to be faithful to you. Guide me by your light as I live out my earthly existence. I look forward to eternal life with you. Amen.

The Light Of Action: Advent is a time of giving. There are many causes to which we can contribute. There are friends, family, and needy strangers for whom we may purchase gifts. There are busy schedules filled with opportunities for fellowship. Yet we must remember that Jesus is the reason for this season. Consider what you will return to the Lord of your time, talents, and stewardship this week. As you do, pray, "Jesus Christ, you are the light of the world. Fill me with your Spirit's love that I might give so others who dwell in darkness may see the light and glorify your Father in heaven. Amen."

Second Week Of Advent

The Light Of The Advent Candle: As you light the second Advent candle, the "Bethlehem Candle," recall the prophet Micah's words, "But you, O Bethlehem of Ephrathah, who are one of the little clans of Judah, from you shall come forth for me one who is to rule in Israel, whose origin is from old, from ancient days" (Micah 5:2).

The Light Of The Word: After lighting the "Bethlehem Candle," read the assigned scripture passage for that day and reflect on the light breaking into the darkness of this world.

Readings For The Second Week In Advent

Sunday: Luke 2:1-7
Key Verse: "Joseph also went from the town of Nazareth in Galilee to Judea, to the city of David called Bethlehem, because he was descended from the house and family of David" (Luke 2:4).
Reflection

Trips can be exciting events. However, Mary was unexpectedly called to go to Bethlehem during the last stage of her pregnancy. It was not a comfortable journey, but she went. In this little town, the city of David, Jesus Christ was born fulfilling the words of the prophet Micah.

How many times does God call us to go where we do not want to go, like attending an extra worship service during Advent? Or how many times does he ask us to do something that we know we should do but don't want to do, like serving in a soup kitchen?

17

Advent is a time to reach out to others and to draw closer to Jesus. Make time in your day for those unexpected things God may call you to do even when they don't seem comfortable.

Prayer

Lord Jesus, thank you for the obedience of your mother, Mary. She put her own comfort behind her in order to do what she had to do. Help me to do likewise. Amen.

Monday: Matthew 2:1-12

Key Verse: "Then he sent them to Bethlehem, saying, 'Go and search diligently for the child; and when you have found him, bring me word so that I may also go and pay him homage' " (Matthew 2:8).

Reflection

The little town of Bethlehem suddenly became an important place in the world. Wise men from the East, who had observed a star, knew that God had done something special. Their studies told them that a new king had come. Herod's scribes and the chief priests searched their records and discovered that Bethlehem would be the site of this king's birth. An insignificant little town became the site of a very significant birth.

Think about the gifts the Magi presented Jesus. What gifts can you bring to him this Advent? What about the gift of self?

Prayer

Lord Jesus, forgive me when I do not feel very significant in your kingdom. Help me to rejoice in all the little things that you call me to do to share your love. Amen.

Tuesday: Luke 2:25-35

Key Verse: "... a light for revelation to the Gentiles and for glory to your people Israel" (Luke 2:32).

Reflection

Israel had long awaited its Messiah, the one who would come as Savior of the world. When Simeon saw Jesus, he knew God had sent that Promised One. The Gentile wise men had seen God's light. Now Israel would behold its glory in a baby.

Jesus came for all people. As we receive him as our Lord and Savior, we can have that peace that Simeon had and not fear death. What does Jesus mean to you? Share your understanding of what salvation is.

Prayer

Lord God, thank you for sending your Son to save me. Amen.

Wednesday: Isaiah 53:10-12

Key Verse: "Out of his anguish he shall see light; he shall find satisfaction through his knowledge. The righteous one, my servant, shall make many righteous, and he shall bear their iniquities" (Isaiah 53:11).

Reflection

Isaiah tells us that God's Anointed would be one who would be called a suffering servant. This one would bear our sins and stand before God in our place.

We see in the suffering of Christ the light of our salvation. He suffered so that we might be made right with God. Consider how much it cost Jesus to do this for sinners.

Prayer

Lord Jesus, you never sinned, yet you took my place as a sinner before God. Thank you for bearing my punishment. Amen.

Thursday: John 9:1-5

Key Verse: "As long as I am in the world, I am the light of the world" (John 9:5).

Reflection

The blinding sun hit the window of the car, causing the driver to lose control of the vehicle momentarily. Quickly pulling the visor down, the driver resumed his course, thanking God that no one was in the other lane.

Sin blinds us to the course we should be following. We have momentary lapses which sometimes cause deep grief and pain. But Jesus is the light which does not blind but opens our eyes to the error of our ways. As long as we keep our eyes on him, we will stay in the right lane in life.

Prayer

Lord Jesus, thank you for touching my eyes and helping me to see those things for which I need to repent. You are my light in this world. Amen.

Friday: John 12:34-36

Key Verse: "While you have the light, believe in the light, so that you may become children of light" (John 12:36).

Reflection

One of the promises made by sponsors at baptism is to faithfully bring the baptized to God's house to worship and to teach them the Lord's Prayer, the Creed, and the Ten Commandments. These precious children of God will then come to believe in Christ. Having seen the light, they become children of the light.

If we do not worship or learn about God, we will find ourselves walking in the darkness of this world. Take time this Advent to add to your spiritual journey by remembering your baptismal vows and putting them into action.

Prayer

Lord Jesus, I come to you as a child and ask you to help me to live in my covenant relationship with you. Amen.

Saturday: John 12:44-47

Key Verse: "I have come as light into the world, so that everyone who believes in me should not remain in the darkness" (John 12:46).

Reflection

The air was heavy with anticipation as the jury returned with the verdict. The judge asked the foreman for their decision. "Not guilty, your honor," came the answer. The defendant's face flooded with joy and relief.

Those who believe in Christ will stand before God on judgment day and hear those same words. Jesus came to save us, and whoever believes in him turns from the darkness of sin to embrace the light of God's grace. Jesus has paid the penalty for our sin. What a joy and relief it will be to stand before God with Christ as our intercessor.

If you were to stand before God today, what would your verdict be?

Prayer

Jesus, thank you for standing before the Father and clearing me of all charges that would condemn me. By faith I receive my pardon through you. Amen.

The Light Of Action: As you consider areas of action in this Advent season, pray, "Holy Child of Bethlehem, you brought the light of love to your parents that night and to those who came to visit you in the lowly stable. Enable me to share that light with my family and all those I come in contact with this week. Receive my humble offering. Amen."

Third Week Of Advent

The Light Of The Advent Candle: As you light the third Advent candle, the "Shepherds' Candle," recall the first shepherds who, having seen the Light lying in a manger that night, went forth rejoicing in their discovery that the Messiah had been born. "The shepherds returned, glorifying and praising God for all they had heard and seen, as it had been told them" (Luke 2:20).

The Light Of The Word: God comes to all people. The shepherds remind us of God's grace and love. They were considered persons of no account in their day. Their testimony was not even valid in a court of law. Yet it was to these humble shepherds that God came to announce the birth of Messiah. When they saw Jesus, they then returned praising God and giving testimony to what they had seen in the light of that stable. As you consider the readings for the week, remember God has come to be your light and calls you to tell others about him.

Readings For The Third Week In Advent

Sunday: Psalm 27:1-4
Key Verse: "The Lord is my light and my salvation; whom shall I fear?" (Psalm 27:1).

21

Reflection

"Own the house of your dreams," the ad in the newspaper said. A picture of a beautiful mansion caused the reader to fantasize about the possibility of living in this architect's temple.

The psalmist tells us that our one desire should be to live in God's house and behold his beauty. The Lord is our light. The Lord is our salvation. As Christians we need not fear where we will go when this life is ended. God has prepared a mansion for us. Yet God calls us to live today in the light of his love and protection. We can be confident that God is with us. This is not a dream but a reality.

Prayer

Holy Spirit, help me to see that you are at work in my life. Continue to light my path and guide me to my eternal home with God. Amen.

Monday: Psalm 104:1-4

Key Verse: "Bless the Lord, O my soul. O Lord my God, you are very great. You are clothed with honor and majesty, wrapped in light as with a garment" (Psalm 104:1-2a).

Reflection

The model, wrapped in a shimmering garment of satin, gracefully strode down the runway. She looked like a princess in this gown of luxury. Her head was held high as she received the laud of those in the audience.

God has clothed each of his children with a beautiful garment of light, salvation in Christ. Let us put that garment on each day as we are wrapped in his love. Clothed in the righteousness of Christ, we become messengers of the Good News and walk proudly as heirs of our King.

Prayer

Holy Spirit, wrap me up in your love. Help me to model the life of Christ in all that I do and to walk proudly in the light of his love. Amen.

Tuesday: Luke 2:8-14

Key Verse: "In that region there were shepherds living in the fields, keeping watch over their flock by night" (Luke 2:8).

Reflection

The darkness of the auditorium was suddenly alive with a dance of lights. Red, yellow, and blue spotlights hit the surfaces of ordinary images, transforming them into splashing visions of color and light.

What a show of lights the shepherds must have beheld that first Christmas night as the host of heaven appeared to announce Jesus' birth. God's messengers come to us today to transform our dark nights, telling us of God's love. Let us eagerly embrace God's light as it comes to us this day in a child wrapped in cloth and lying in a manger.

Prayer

Holy Spirit, thank you for showing me signs of your activity in my world. Help me not to be terrified but to have joy in the knowledge that you are in control. Amen.

Wednesday: Luke 2:15-20

Key Verse: "The shepherds returned, glorifying and praising God for all they had heard and seen, as it had been told them" (Luke 2:20).

Reflection

Act 1 Scene 1: The darkness is dispelled by the light of the heavenly host. Angels come to earth to announce tidings of great joy. Praise to God is offered up.

Act 1 Scene 2: Angels depart stage left. Shepherds head to Bethlehem and find Mary, Joseph, and the baby. Excitedly they share what has been revealed to them.

Act 1 Scene 3: Shepherds return to the fields having found the true light of the world, rejoicing in the Good News of salvation.

Act 1 Scene 4: The light has dawned on us. We praise and rejoice in finding Jesus in our midst. Where will we go to share the Good News?

Prayer

Holy Spirit, each day brings another opportunity to witness to my faith in Christ. Help me not to be terrified about the prospect but to rejoice in every chance. Amen.

Thursday: Luke 8:16-17

Key Verse: "No one after lighting a lamp hides it under a jar, or puts it under a bed, but puts it on a lampstand, so that those who enter may see the light" (Luke 8:16).

Reflection

The camp was in darkness. "Someone find the kerosene lamp," a voice called out. "We need a match." A light flickered as the mantle of the lamp caught fire. Soon a flame burned brightly. The lamp was placed on the table. The room became a cozy place flooded with light.

The lamp would have done our campers no good if it had been shoved into a closet. Our knowledge of who Jesus is does others no good if we do not share it. How might you show others that you have come to know Jesus as your Lord?

Prayer

Holy Spirit, I need you to strike the fire of evangelism in my soul. Help me to share my knowledge of Jesus with others. Amen.

Friday: 2 Corinthians 4:3-6

Key Verse: "For it is the God who said, 'Let light shine out of darkness,' who has shone in our hearts to give the light of the knowledge of the glory of God in the face of Jesus Christ" (2 Corinthians 4:6).

Reflection

"You saw the President of the United States? Fat chance. We don't believe you."

The students in the classroom hooted at Justin's remark about having seen the President.

"But I did! I did! You have to believe me."

Justin had seen the President when he had visited the White House on a tour. However, his classmates' minds were veiled in unbelief that this small town boy could have actually seen such an important person.

We have not seen Jesus in the flesh as the shepherds did, but we do see Jesus with eyes of faith as the Holy Spirit reveals him to us through the Word, through prayer, in worship, and in fellowship with other believers. It is this Christ we see that we proclaim to an unbelieving world. Let God's light shine upon your hearts so that you can behold the face of Jesus more fully this Advent season.

Prayer

Holy Spirit, continue to reveal Christ as Lord and open the blinded minds of unbelievers to your light. Amen.

Saturday: Ephesians 5:8-14

Key Verse: "For everything that becomes visible is light. Therefore it says, 'Sleeper, awake! Rise from the dead, and Christ will shine on you' " (Ephesians 5:14).

Reflection

"All right, you bunch of dead sleepers. Rise and shine. It's time to expose yourselves to a new day," the sergeant's voice boomed out to his men in the barracks.

When the light of Christ shines upon us, we awaken to new life. We cannot continue to live as children of the dark, dead in our sins. Christ's light exposes the sin we have engaged in and calls us to turn away from it. As children of the light, we now live differently. Advent is a good time to look at the fruit of your life. Is it good and right and true?

Prayer

Holy Spirit, you called me out of the darkness into the light by revealing who Jesus is to me. Help me to live as his child and to walk in obedience to his call. Amen.

The Light Of Action: As Mary gave her consent to have Christ born in her, let this Advent season be one in which you say "Yes" to God's call on your life. Mary gave the Holy Spirit permission to move in her life, and she was blessed. The shepherds could have stayed home that night and would have missed out on the greatest blessing of their lives — seeing the Christ Child. They responded to God's call to go and find the baby, and they were blessed. Today the Holy Spirit will speak to you concerning Jesus' plan for your life. When you embrace the light of God's love and respond in all areas of your life, especially in your actions, you, too, will be blessed. Each day ask the Holy Spirit to help you pray, "Great Shepherd, having grasped the knowledge of who you are — the Light of Salvation — enable me to go out like those first shepherds to be a witness to others of that revelation. May my humble actions spread that Good News so that others may know of your love. Amen."

Fourth Week Of Advent

The Light Of The Advent Candle: As you light the fourth Advent candle, the "Angels' Candle," recall the heavenly messengers who came to announce the birth of the Christ Child. "And suddenly there was with the angel a multitude of the heavenly host, praising God and saying, 'Glory to God in the highest heaven, and on earth peace among those whom he favors!' " (Luke 2:13-14).

The Light Of The Word: Angels are messengers sent by God. Today there is quite a fascination with these heavenly beings. But they are not the ones that should fascinate us. It is the message they bring — the message from God — that should stir our curiosity, disturb us when we find ourselves too comfortable, and comfort us in our afflictions. This week recall the message the angels delivered, "Salvation has come. The Light of God's love has been revealed. Run to the stable and see your salvation." With eagerness and joy approach the manger and the end of this Advent season.

Readings For The Fourth Week In Advent

Sunday: Luke 1:26-33
Key Verse: "In the sixth month the angel Gabriel was sent by God to a town in Galilee called Nazareth" (Luke 1:26).

Reflection

In this final week of Advent, we receive many lovely Christmas cards from family and friends. These cards bring greetings from home to home. Some cards show shepherds in their fields; some show the wise men following a star; others are decorated with a wide assortment of angels. The angel that came to Mary was not the typical Christmas card angel with long, flowing dress and trumpet. This was Gabriel, a messenger sent straight from the throne room of God. Gabriel had the honor of serving the Almighty and being entrusted to deliver this most important bit of news.

As this angel had God's favor and trust, recall how Mary had gained God's favor also. What does God's favor mean? Share how you might find favor with this Almighty God who sends his trusted messengers to tell us of Jesus.

Prayer

Almighty God, you bring me tidings of great joy this Advent season. Remind me to have ears to hear what your Spirit is saying to my heart. Amen.

Monday: Hebrews 1:1-4

Key Verse: "... having become as much superior to angels as the name he has inherited is more excellent than theirs" (Hebrews 1:4).

Reflection

Watching muscle builders on television, we might consider them physically superior to us as human beings. When we think of angels, we think of them as superior beings. Yet the writer of the Book of Hebrews tells us that Jesus, the Son of Man, is superior to them.

The Child of Bethlehem grew up and became a man. He then suffered death but was raised to life once more. Then he ascended to the right hand of God. The angels surround his throne now singing his praises as once they sang on that first Christmas night.

As we approach Christmas Day, let us continue to raise our voices in praise along with God's angels and sing of the joy we have found in Jesus, the most superior to all beings.

Prayer

Almighty God, I behold your majesty in all of your creations. Thank you for sustaining me through your Word. Amen.

Tuesday: Hebrews 1:5-9

Key Verse: "For to which of the angels did God ever say, 'You are my Son; today I have begotten you'?" (Hebrews 1:5).

Reflection

Angels are God's created beings. Jesus is God's Son. Angels are spiritual entities resembling God in nature. Jesus is the exact imprint of God's being. Angels worship him, for he is the begotten one of God. Jesus is God's anointed. There are millions of these created beings in heaven, yet Jesus is superior to this vast number of angelic beings which surround the throne of grace. Jesus is God's grace.

Let the light of God's love and grace shine into your final week of Advent. Worship Jesus along with the angels, for he truly deserves our worship and praise. Remember it is Jesus, the one and only Son of God, whose glory the angels sing.

Prayer

Almighty God, I lift my praise to your Son, Jesus. Establish his throne in my heart as I pay homage to him as my Lord and King. Amen.

Wednesday: Hebrews 2:5-9

Key Verse: "But we do see Jesus, who for a little while was made lower than the angels, now crowned with glory and honor because of the suffering of death, so that by the grace of God he might taste death for everyone" (Hebrews 2:9).

Reflection

"Come on down!" the announcer on the game show cries out. "You're the next contestant on *The Price Is Right!*" Eagerly a contestant races down the aisle to take his place, hoping to win the next prize.

God called Jesus to come down to earth and for a time to become lower than the angels. He became a contestant in the battle over sin and death. He won the prize — salvation — and has secured it for us as his children with the price of his life.

Remember the wood of the manger this Advent. Life came into the world and was placed in wood. That life would be placed upon another wood and find death. It is upon the wood of a Cross that Jesus paid the price of our salvation. Yet he offers that salvation free of charge. He only asks that we believe and "come on down" to meet him as Lord.

Prayer

Almighty God, help me to become humble as your Son Jesus did. As you crowned him with glory, crown me with grace so I can receive the prize of my salvation. Amen.

Thursday: 1 Thessalonians 5:4-10

Key Verse: "For you are all children of light and children of the day; we are not of the night or of darkness" (1 Thessalonians 5:5).

Reflection

The evening headlines warned, "Don't Go into the City at Night!" All across the nation people are being warned to stay out of areas where the children of the dark are preying upon the innocent. Crime is on the upsurge in our cities across the nation, and the perpetrators seem to get away with their evil deeds. At times we wonder if people ever pay the consequences of their violent actions. What about the innocent victims?

God does not want us to be innocent about sin and its consequences. The wrath of God will be poured out on those who do evil. God sees and will render his final verdict on those who continue to live in rebellion to his love. As children of the light, we are to trust God wherever we may venture, clothed in his love and protection. So whether asleep or awake we have no need to fear, for God is with us.

Prayer

Almighty God, I ask forgiveness for not trusting in you to take care of those who do their deeds in the darkness. I pray for them to come to the light of your love. Amen.

Friday: 1 John 1:5-7

Key Verse: "This is the message we have heard from him and proclaim to you, that God is light and in him there is no darkness at all" (1 John 1:5).

Reflection

"The light's burned out in the closet again, and I can't find my mittens," a child hollered in frustration. "Someone bring me a light bulb!"

God is light. When we are walking with him, we live in harmony with one another. However, if we have chosen to let his love burn out in our hearts by not cultivating it, we will live out life groping around in the dark not being able to find our way let alone our mittens.

Advent is a time to examine our relationship with God. His light will reveal the true nature of our hearts. Think about how you live with those around you. If there is reconciliation to be done, allow God to move you to do it so that you can find peace. Clean your closets of any resentments that might be hanging about. Turn the light of forgiveness on bright. Turn to Christ and receive your peace.

Prayer

Almighty God, I hear your message to put aside old grudges and hurt feelings. Help me to be at peace with others so that I can be at peace with myself and you. Amen.

Saturday: Revelation 22:1-5

Key Verse: "And there will be no more night; they need no light of lamp or sun, for the Lord God will be their light, and they will reign forever and ever." (Revelation 22:5).

Reflection

The science project was a success. The African violet had grown healthy and flowered brightly as it had been exposed to perpetual light.

As we are exposed to the light of Christ, we will grow healthy and bear the flower of a faith rooted and grounded in him. But we are not to be hothouse plants, sitting in one spot and taking in light from a grow lamp. God has called us to travel through the darkness of this life being lights to others as we follow him. At those times when we feel the darkness might overcome us, we need to remember that when we reach our heavenly home, there will be no more night. God will be our perpetual light, and we will reign with him forever. As the light of Christmas now breaks into our world once again, we long for Christ's return. We long to hear God's message declaring that Christ is on his way to take us home. Then we will see him face to face. And so we end our Advent journey as we began it, by asking Jesus, "O come, Blessed Light of the World!"

Prayer

Almighty God, I long for your return. Give me patience to wait faithfully until your Son comes back with the angels to take me home to be forever with you. Amen.

The Light Of Action: God's message still rings out in our world. He has sent his messengers to all corners of the earth declaring the Good News of salvation for all people. Consider areas of mission that you might support in your congregation, your community, and in the world. Then pray, "Almighty God, you sent your messengers to Mary and to the shepherds to proclaim the Light entering our world. Empower me to go forth with the message of salvation I have received through your Son, Jesus Christ my Lord. Use my actions as messengers of love to others. Amen."

CONclUsioN

As the light of Christmas comes to the world once more, remember all you have learned in this Advent season of God's love and light. Reflect that understanding in all you do and say. Let the Father, the Son, and the Holy Spirit continue to guide and direct you. Do not stop with Christmas, but continue your journey of faith as you pray each day of your life, "O come, Blessed Light of the World!"

May the light of God's love guide and direct you each day of your new life in Christ.

31

Celebrating The Advent Wreath
A Special Advent Service

Jesus Is The Light

Introductory Remarks (Leader)
A Reading from the Gospel: John 1:1-15
Evergreens
Opening Hymn: "On Jordan's Banks" (vv. 1, 2, 5)
Optional Homily

The Advent Wreath

The First Candle: The Prophecy Candle
First Reading: Isaiah 7:14; Matthew 1:18-23
Reflection on the First Candle
Hymn: "What Child Is This?"

The Second Candle: The Bethlehem Candle
Second Reading: Micah 5:2; Luke 2:1-7
Reflection on the Second Candle
Hymn: "O Little Town Of Bethlehem"

The Third Candle: The Shepherds' Candle
Third Reading: Luke 2:8-20
Reflection on the Third Candle
Hymn: "The First Noel" (v. 1)

The Fourth Candle: The Angels' Candle
Fourth Reading: Luke 1:26-38
Reflection on the Fourth Candle
Hymn: "Hark! The Herald Angels Sing"

Collection of Offering

The Celebration Of Holy Communion

The Fifth Candle: The Christ Candle
Reflection on the Fifth Candle
Words of Institution
The Lord's Prayer
Distribution of Communion

The Blessing

Leader: Now may the blessing of Jesus Christ, the expected one, the one whose birth we celebrate once again, be upon us as we hail the Christ Child our Redeemer and King. Go forth into the night remembering the silence of that first Holy Night. In the name of the Father, the Son, and the Holy Spirit.
Congregation: Amen.
Closing Hymn: "Silent Night"

Celebrating The Advent Wreath
A Special Advent Service

Jesus Is The Light

Introductory Remarks (Leader)

The Church celebrates the season of Advent as a time of preparation. The word "advent" means "coming" or "arrival." Advent for Christians is a time of preparing for the arrival of God's Son into our hearts. During the four Sundays of Advent many churches make use of the Advent Wreath. These wreaths are in the form of a circle. Circles have no end. Eternity is like the circle, and our life with God reflects this. Eternal life is for us, when we die, an everlasting reward. Yet our eternal life begins in our baptism, when we were made children of God. It continues in the present as we surrender to the lordship of Jesus Christ, and it will always be with us because we believe and have faith in God's Son.

The four candles in our wreath represent the four weeks of preparation in Advent during which we are mindful of our need to recognize the true light of the world. Hear what the Word of God says concerning that light.

A Reading from the Gospel: John 1:1-15

Evergreens

The Advent Wreath is often covered with evergreen boughs. Evergreens also symbolize eternal life. Green is the color associated with life and growth. In our life of faith, we have a responsibility to grow. We do this through prayer, the study of God's Word, corporate and private worship, and fellowship with other believers. New life is ours through our relationship with Jesus Christ. The Holy Spirit is the one who reveals Christ to us. We are reconciled to the source of life as we confess our sins and receive God's mercy found in Christ. John the Baptist came calling Israel to repent. Let us begin our program of worship by singing "On Jordan's Banks The Baptist's Cry."

35

Opening Hymn: "On Jordan's Banks" (vv. 1, 2, 5)
Optional Homily

The Advent Wreath

The First Candle: The Prophecy Candle
First Reading: Isaiah 7:14; Matthew 1:18-23
Reflection on the First Candle

The first candle we light has been called the *Prophecy Candle*. This candle reminds us of the prophets who spoke of the coming of the Messiah, the Anointed One of God, who would come to bless his people. Our reading from Isaiah tells us that the Lord would give his people a sign. This sign would be of a virgin who would be with child. She would give birth to a son and would call him Immanuel, which means "God with us." The Gospel text tells us that this prophecy was fulfilled with the union of God's Spirit and the open vessel, Mary. As we light our first candle, let us consider this child born of Mary by singing "What Child Is This?" *(First candle is lit during the singing of the hymn.)*
Hymn: "What Child Is This?"

The Second Candle: The Bethlehem Candle
Second Reading: Micah 5:2; Luke 2:1-7
Reflection on the Second Candle

The second candle we light is called the *Bethlehem Candle*. The prophet Micah spoke of the birth of God's Messiah 700 years before Jesus was actually born. This ruler would be born in the city of David, Bethlehem. This passage shows us the awesomeness of God's arrangements. In order to get Joseph and Mary to Bethlehem, God placed it upon Caesar's heart to take a census. So Mary and Joseph had to travel from Nazareth to Bethlehem to register. God would place them in the right spot to fulfill Micah's prophecy. As we light this second candle, consider how God is in control of every detail of our lives as we sing "O Little Town Of Bethlehem." *(Light second candle while hymn is sung.)*
Hymn: "O Little Town Of Bethlehem"

The Third Candle: The Shepherds' Candle
Third Reading: Luke 2:8-20
Reflection on the Third Candle

Candle number three has been called the *Shepherds' Candle*. This candle reminds us of the first witnesses who heard the Good News. Upon hearing it, they ran with joy and anticipation to see this Savior born in Bethlehem. We rejoice that Christ came to lowly shepherds, for that means salvation is not for a select few but is a gift given to all people. We have access to God when we humble ourselves before the manger and embrace God's love born in a little child. Jesus came as the Good Shepherd to guide us into the Father's love. He bore witness to that love with his death upon the Cross. We bear witness to God's love as we share Christ's love in community with others. As we light our third candle, let us witness our faith in Christ as we sing of that first Christmas night with the carol "The First Noel." (*Light third candle while hymn is sung.*)
Hymn: "The First Noel" (v. 1)

The Fourth Candle: The Angels' Candle
Fourth Reading: Luke 1:26-38
Reflection on the Fourth Candle

Our fourth candle, called the *Angels' Candle*, symbolizes the messengers of God who came from heaven to announce the birth of our Lord and Savior. Over the years interest in the angels has become a hot topic. Angels have a ministry to mortals of protection and loving care. The angel Gabriel came to Mary with a very special message. She had found favor with God and, if willing to be open to God's Spirit, would conceive and bear God's Son. As we light our fourth candle, let us be like Mary, believing in God to fulfill his promises to us, yielding to his will for our lives, submitting ourselves to the care of a loving God, and being open to trust God in every area of our lives. Our offering will be taken as we call upon God's angels to come and be with us as we sing "Hark! The Herald Angels Sing." (*Fourth candle is lighted during singing of hymn.*)
Hymn: "Hark! The Herald Angels Sing"
Collection of Offering

The Celebration Of Holy Communion

The Fifth Candle: The Christ Candle
Reflection on the Fifth Candle
  On Christmas Eve, a fifth candle is lit. This candle, placed in the center of the circle, is the *Christ Candle*. It tells us that the One who is the light of our darkness has been born. We will celebrate that light tonight by sharing in the sacrament of Holy Communion. Hear the Words of Institution and recall God's love poured out in Christ's sacrifice for the redemption of the world.
Words of Institution
The Lord's Prayer
Distribution of Communion

The Blessing

Leader: Now may the blessing of Jesus Christ, the expected one, the one whose birth we celebrate once again, be upon us as we hail the Christ Child our Redeemer and King. Go forth into the night remembering the silence of that first Holy Night. In the name of the Father, the Son, and the Holy Spirit.
Congregation: Amen.
Closing Hymn: "Silent Night"

Symbols

ChRisTMAs Symbols ANd SoNqs

Program Participants:
Leader
Reader 1: Isaiah 7:14
Reader 2: Isaiah 11:1-3
Reader 3: Isaiah 9:2-7
Reader 4: Matthew 1:18-25

Props:
Candle, straw, grapes, wheat, pomegranate, mistletoe, bare branch, star, evergreens, holly and berries, palm, red rose, fern, dove, wreath, pine cone, ivy, holly, small artificial Christmas tree, Jesus symbol (cross)

Optional:
It may be desirable to create song sheets with the printed words of each of the Christmas songs for easy use by the worshiping group. Hymnals or songbooks may be used. For the Christmas songs which are no longer found in hymnals, the words may either be printed on song sheets or included in the bulletin.

PROGRAM

CHRISTMAS Symbols And Songs

Leader: Christmas decorations! Already we see them in the stores, restaurants, and homes. One of the songs used to deck one's rooms for the season is the traditional Welsh carol, "Deck The Halls." As greens were being hung and the house decorated, it was the custom to leave the outer doors of the house unbolted so that the Holy Family might enter in. Candles, which symbolize Christ as the Light of the World, were lit to welcome our Lord into the homes and hearts once again. Let us begin our program tonight by lighting a **candle** and throwing open the doors of our hearts as we sing "Deck The Halls."

Song: "Deck The Halls"
Deck the halls with boughs of holly,
Fa, la, la, la, la, la, la, la, la.
'Tis the season to be jolly,
Fa, la, la, la, la, la, la, la, la.
Don we now our gay apparel,
Fa, la, la, la, la, la, la, la, la.
Troll the ancient Yuletide carol,
Fa, la, la, la, la, la, la, la, la.

See the blazing Yule before us,
Fa, la, la, la, la, la, la, la, la.
Strike the harp and join the chorus,
Fa, la, la, la, la, la, la, la, la.
Follow me in merry measure,
Fa, la, la, la, la, la, la, la, la.
While I tell of Yuletide treasure,
Fa, la, la, la, la, la, la, la, la.

Fast away the old year passes,
Fa, la, la, la, la, la, la, la, la.

42

Hail the new, ye lads and lasses,
Fa, la, la, la, la, la, la, la, la.
Sing we joyous all together,
Fa, la, la, la, la, la, la, la, la.
Heedless of the wind and weather,
Fa, la, la, la, la, la, la, la, la.

Leader: It is cold for many at Christmas. For animals outside, this symbol, **straw**, is one which helps them stay warm, dry, and comfortable. Straw is symbolic of the manger and Christ's humble birth. Straw is dried hay, a feed for animals. Some other edible items which are symbols of the season are **grapes**, symbolizing the wine of Holy Communion and the blood of Christ; **wheat**, symbolizing the bread of Holy Communion and the human nature of Jesus; and the **pomegranate**, which represents the Tomb. Broken, this fruit illustrates the miracle of Christ's resurrection. It has also become a symbol of the church because of the inner unity of its countless seeds in one and the same fruit. As we reflect on these symbols, let us journey back to that manger where our Lord Jesus first laid his small head.

Song: "Away In A Manger"
Away in a manger, no crib for a bed,
The little Lord Jesus laid down his sweet head;
The stars in the sky looked down where he lay,
The little Lord Jesus asleep on the hay.

The cattle are lowing, the poor baby wakes,
But little Lord Jesus no crying he makes.
I love thee, Lord Jesus! Look down from the sky,
And stay by my cradle till morning is nigh.

Be near me, Lord Jesus; I ask thee to stay
Close by me forever and love me, I pray;
Bless all the dear children in thy tender care,
And take us to heaven, to live with thee there.

Leader: As we journey into the woods to find decorations for our homes, we might come upon some **mistletoe**, the symbol of peace, or into an orchard and find **bare fruit branches**, symbolic of the hope of the world for its salvation. The child, born in the stable, would be called the Prince of Peace. We hail the babe, the son of Mary, the hope of our world and our salvation.

Song: "What Child Is This?"
What child is this, who, laid to rest,
On Mary's lap is sleeping?
Whom angels greet with anthems sweet
While shepherds watch are keeping?
This, this is Christ the king,
Whom shepherds guard and angels sing;
Haste, haste to bring him laud,
The babe, the son of Mary!

Why lies he in such mean estate
Where ox and ass are feeding?
Good Christian, fear; for sinners here
The silent Word is pleading.
Nails, spear shall pierce him through,
The cross be borne for me, for you;
Hail, hail the Word made flesh,
The babe, the son of Mary!

So bring him incense, gold, and myrrh;
Come, peasant, king, to own him.
The King of kings salvation brings;
Let loving hearts enthrone him.
Raise, raise the song on high,
The virgin sings her lullaby;
Joy, joy, for Christ is born,
The babe, the son of Mary!

Leader: Yes, the Son of Mary, the Son of God, is the King of kings. And the star that shone that first night, the **star**, which is symbolic of divine guidance and foretells the coming of the Babe of Bethlehem, appeared and guided three sages from the East to meet their Lord. Let us journey with them in song.

Song: "We Three Kings"
We three kings of Orient are;
Bearing gifts we traverse afar,
Field and fountain, moor and mountain,
Following yonder star.

Refrain:
O star of wonder, star of night,
Star with royal beauty bright,
Westward leading, still proceeding,
Guide us to thy perfect light.

Born a King on Bethlehem's plain,
Gold I bring, to crown him again,
King forever, ceasing never,
Over us all to reign. *(Refrain)*

Frankincense to offer have I,
Incense owns a Deity nigh,
Pray'r and praising, all men raising,
Worship him, God most high. *(Refrain)*

Myrrh is mine, its bitter perfume
Breathes a life of gathering gloom;
Sorrowing, sighing, bleeding, dying,
Seal'd in the stone-cold tomb. *(Refrain)*

Glorious now behold him arise,
King and God and sacrifice;
Alleluia, alleluia,
Earth to the heav'ns replies. *(Refrain)*

Leader: But let's go out into nature again and look at some more Christmas symbols. **Evergreens** represent Christ's triumph over adversity and death and are symbolic of eternal life. **Holly and berries** represent Christ's crown of thorns and his drops of blood. The **palm** symbolizes victory and is a reminder of the flight of the holy family into Egypt, Christ's triumphant entry into Jerusalem, and his victory over sin and death. **Red roses** symbolize God's divine love and the martyrdom of his Son. The **fern** is symbolic of the Word. Fresh fern reminds us of the new teaching of Christ while dried fern symbolizes the Old Testament teachings. Our next song, "Lo, How A Rose Is Growing," hails the Rose of Sharon, the branch of Jesse of the house of King David, the one told about in the Old Testament and the Word made flesh in the New.

Song: "Lo, How A Rose Is Growing"
Lo, how a rose is growing,
A bloom of finest grace;
The prophets had foretold it:
A branch of Jesse's race
Would bear one perfect flow'r
Here in the cold of winter
And darkest midnight hour.

The rose of which I'm singing,
Isaiah had foretold.
He came to us through Mary
Who sheltered him from cold.
Through God's eternal will
This child to us was given
At midnight calm and still.

This flow'r, so small and tender,
With fragrance fills the air;
His brightness ends the darkness
That kept the earth in fear.
True God and yet true man,
He came to save his people
From earth's dark night of sin.

Leader: Hear what the prophet Isaiah foretold:

Reader: Isaiah 7:14 and Isaiah 11:1-3

Leader: A child would be born of the house of David. But this child would not be born in a palace, but in a stable. Let us hear of that child.

Song: "Infant Holy, Infant Lowly"
Infant holy, infant lowly,
For his bed a cattle stall;
Oxen lowing, little knowing
Christ the child is Lord of all.
Swiftly winging, angels singing,
Bells are ringing, tidings bringing;
Christ the child is Lord of all!
Christ the child is Lord of all!

Flocks were sleeping,
Shepherds keeping
Vigil till the morning new
Saw the glory, heard the story,
Tidings of a Gospel true.
Thus rejoicing, free from sorrow,
Praises voicing, greet the morrow.
Christ the child was born for you!
Christ the child was born for you!

Leader: And the prophet told what that child would be named. Hear again from Isaiah.

Reader: Isaiah 9:2-7

Leader: And hear about the conception and the birth of Jesus.

Reader: Matthew 1:18-25

Leader: The final objects are before us. The **wreath** symbolizes Christ's unending, unwavering faith and represents immortality. **Pine cones** tell us of the seed of faith, sown by Christ. And the **ivy** is the symbol of God, immortality, and fidelity. The **holly** was originally the Holy Tree. The traditional French carol, "The Holly And The Ivy," suggests the importance attached to that object during this season. It is supposed to have sprung up for the first time beneath the footsteps of Christ when he first walked on earth.

Song: "The Holly And The Ivy"
The holly and the ivy, now both are full well grown,
Of all the trees within the wood, the holly bears the crown.

Refrain:
O the rising of the sun, the running of the deer,
The playing of the merry organ,
Sweet singing in the choir, sweet singing in the choir.

The holly bears a blossom, as white as any flow'r,
And Mary bore sweet Jesus Christ, to be our sweet Savior.
(*Refrain*)

The holly bears a berry, as red as any blood,
And Mary bore sweet Jesus Christ, to do poor sinners good.
(*Refrain*)

The holly bears a prickle, as sharp as any thorn,
And Mary bore sweet Jesus Christ, On Christmas Day in the morn.
(*Refrain*)

Leader: Many people have already put up their **Christmas tree** or will do it soon. There is a legend surrounding this object of Christmas also. It seems that one clear, cold Christmas Eve, a man was walking through the snow on his way home. As he looked up through the branches of the evergreens along the way, he saw hundreds of stars twinkling like silver jewels. Enthralled, he wanted

48

to share this beauty he saw with his small, invalid daughter. Hurrying home, he fetched his ax to cut down a lovely tree. Taking it into his house, he decorated it with lighted candles so that his child would know something of the beauty of the stars shining through the branches of the trees that he had seen. As he brought the child into the room, she gasped in delight. It was almost as if the light of heaven was within their small home. She hugged him, and together they thanked God for their Savior. Today the twinkling lights on our tree remind us of the Light from heaven above.

Song: "O Christmas Tree"
O Christmas Tree, O Christmas Tree,
Your branches green delight us.
O Christmas Tree, O Christmas Tree,
Your branches green delight us.
They're green when summer days are bright;
They're green when winter snow is white.
O Christmas Tree, O Christmas Tree,
Your branches green delight us.

O Christmas Tree, O Christmas Tree,
You give us so much pleasure!
O Christmas Tree, O Christmas Tree,
You give us so much pleasure!
How oft at Christmastide the sight,
O green fir tree, gives us delight!
O Christmas Tree, O Christmas Tree,
You give us so much pleasure.

Leader: All the symbols of this season give us great pleasure. But let us not forget the one to whom they point: **Jesus**, the Christ Child, the one whom we adore. Let us close our program tonight by standing and singing "O Come, All Ye Faithful." Let us adore Christ, our Lord.

Song: "O Come, All Ye Faithful"
O come, all ye faithful, joyful and triumphant,
O come ye, O come ye to Bethlehem,
Come and behold him, born the king of angels;

Refrain:
O come let us adore him,
O come let us adore him,
O come let us adore him,
Christ the Lord.

Sing, choirs of angels,
Sing in exultation,
Sing, all ye citizens of heav'n above:
Glory to God in the highest; *(Refrain)*

Yea, Lord, we greet thee,
Born this happy morning;
Jesus, to Thee be glory giv'n,
Word of the Father now in flesh appearing; *(Refrain)*

Leader: Go in the peace of the Christ Child and be filled with the
Christmas spirit. Go in peace. Serve the Lord.
C: Thanks be to God!

Angels

Angels Inspire Our Worship

Worship Leader
Angel Litany: Angel 1, Angel 2, Angel 3, Angel 4, Angel 5
Readers: Revelation 22:1-7; Psalm 103:19-22; Luke 2:1-14
Angels Appear in the Old and New Testaments: Reader 1, Reader 2, Reader 3, Reader 4
Special Music: "The Little Drummer Boy" or another selection
Prayer Leader: Prayer of the Church and The Lord's Prayer

Hark! It's Harold And The Angel Band
Skit

Props:
One street sign with a large cloud on it. Written on one side, "Heaven." Use in Scene 1. Turn around in Scene 2, "Heaven's Grocery Store."
Table with groceries on it, box of "Sweet & Low," paper sacks and plastic carry-out carts.
Have song sheets for Angel Choir.

Angel Choir:
Leader: Harold
3 Speaking Angels
Choir may have tambourines, clickers, shakers, and so on. Angel 1 carries a harp or autoharp. Angel 2 carries a guitar.

Scene 1: Group dresses in white robes with haloes (gold garland).
Scene 2: Group wears street clothes.

Main Characters:
Mr. Grumpy and Mr. Grumpier (dress as old men in flannel shirts with hats)
Gabe the Stock Boy (wears an apron)

Angels Inspire Our Worship
Mid-week Advent Worship Service

Call To Worship
L: As the angels appeared in the heavens proclaiming Messiah's birth, let us now come and worship Jesus the Christ, our heavenly king.

C: Come, worship Jesus the King!

Song: "Angels From The Realms Of Glory"
Angels, from the realms of glory,
Wing your flight o'er all the earth;
Once you sang creation's story;
Now proclaim Messiah's birth:

Refrain:
Come and worship, come and worship,
Worship Christ, the newborn king.

Shepherds, in the fields abiding,
Watching o'er your flocks by night,
God with us is now residing,
Yonder shines the infant light. (*Refrain*)

Sages, leave your contemplations,
Brighter visions beam afar;
Seek the great desire of nations,
You have seen his natal star. (*Refrain*)

All creation, join in praising
God, the Father, Spirit, Son,
Evermore your voices raising
To the eternal Three in One. (*Refrain*)

Angel Litany

Angel 1: I am an angel sent by God to serve those who will inherit salvation.

C: The angels rejoice when one sinner repents.

Angel 2: I am an angel, immortal. I stand before God and praise Jesus.

C: As mortals we stand in God's presence through Jesus, our Lord.

Angel 3: I am an angel, and I am concerned about human things.

C: Lord, raise our concern for others.

Angel 4: I am an angel sent by God to spread the Good News.

C: Holy Spirit, open our ears to the salvation message.

Angel 5: I am an angel who sings in the heavenly choir.

C: We join the choirs of angels worshiping Christ, the newborn King.

Prayer Of The Day
L: Almighty God, you have created and established a great order for the ministries of angels and mortals. In your mercy grant that those holy angels, who are always ready to serve and worship you in heaven, will by your appointment assist and defend us here on earth; through your Son, Jesus Christ, our Lord, who lives and reigns with you and the Holy Spirit, one God, now and forever.
C: Amen.

Song: "Oh, Come, All Ye Faithful"
Oh, come, all ye faithful, Joyful and triumphant!
Oh, come ye, oh, come ye to Bethlehem;
Come and behold him Born the king of angels:

Refrain:
Oh, come, let us adore him,
Oh, come, let us adore him,
Oh, come, let us adore him, Christ the Lord!

The highest, most holy, Light of light eternal,
Born of a virgin, a mortal he comes;
Son of the Father Now in flesh appearing! *(Refrain)*

Sing, choirs of angels, Sing in exultation,
Sing, all ye citizens of heaven above!
Glory to God In the highest: *(Refrain)*

Yea, Lord, we greet thee, Born this happy morning;
Jesus, to thee be glory giv'n!
Word of the Father, Now in flesh appearing: *(Refrain)*

First Lesson: Revelation 22:1-7

Psalm 103:1-5, 19-22 (Read responsively)
L: Bless the Lord, O my soul, and all that is within me, bless his holy name.

C: Bless the Lord, O my soul, and do not forget all God's benefits.

L: Who forgives all your iniquity, who heals all your diseases,

C: Who redeems your life from the pit, who crowns you with steadfast love and mercy,

L: Who satisfies you with good as long as you live so that your youth is renewed like an eagle's.

C: The Lord has established his throne in the heavens, and his kingdom rules over all.

L: Bless the Lord, O you his angels, you mighty ones who do his bidding, obedient to his spoken word.

C: Bless the Lord, all his hosts, his ministers that do his will.

L: Bless the Lord, all his works, in all places of his dominion.

C: Bless the Lord, O my soul. Amen.

Angels Appear In The Old Testament

Reader 1: Behold! God's angels appeared to many in the Old Testament: to Abraham to tell him he would have a son in his old age; to Hagar to rescue her in the desert and give her knowledge that God saw her distress; to Lot to lead him from evil Sodom; to Jacob on a ladder ascending and descending from heaven; to Moses in a burning bush; to Joshua as the divine commander of the Lord's army; to Gideon as he was threshing wheat; to David as an agent of doom; to Zechariah as a wall of fire around Jerusalem. Many were the visits of God through angels in the Old Testament.

C: Praise God for the ministry of angels!

Angels Appear In The New Testament

Reader 2: Behold! God's angels came also to those of the New Testament with hope, promise, and deliverance — to Zechariah and Mary to announce the birth of a son; to Joseph to give him reassurance that Mary's child was God's son; to the shepherds announcing Christ's birth; to Mary Magdalene and her companions in the garden tomb; to the apostles at Christ's ascension; to Peter in jail; to Philip on a desert road; to Cornelius to announce salvation to the Gentiles; to Paul on board a ship; to John of Patmos in visions. Many were the visits of God announcing Good News through the angels in the New Testament.

C: Praise God for the ministry of angels!

Reader 3: Angels had a ministry in Christ's life. They announced his conception. They heralded his birth. After the devil had tempted him in the wilderness, they sustained him. They witnessed and proclaimed his resurrection from the dead. And they accompanied him to heaven. Many were the visits of God to his Son through the angels.

C: Praise God for the ministry of angels!

Reader 4: As angels came in the Old and New Testaments, so angels are sent to the earth today. May we become more aware of God's visits among us and of his angels in our midst.

C: Praise God for the ministry of angels!

Song: "It Came Upon The Midnight Clear" (vv. 1, 2)
It came upon the midnight clear,
That glorious song of old,
From angels bending near the earth
To touch their harps of gold:
"Peace on the earth, good will to all,
From heav'n's all-gracious king."
The world in solemn stillness lay
To hear the angels sing.

58

Still through the cloven skies they come
With peaceful wings unfurled,
And still their heav'nly music floats
O'er all the weary world.
Above its sad and lowly plains
They bend on hov'ring wing.
And ever o'er its babel sounds
The blessed angels sing.

Gospel Reading: Luke 2:1-14

Song: "It Came Upon the Midnight Clear" (vv. 3, 4)
And you, beneath life's crushing load,
Whose forms are bending low,
Who toil along the climbing way
With painful steps and slow:
Look now, for glad and golden hours
Come swiftly on the wing;
Oh, rest beside the weary road
And hear the angels sing!

For lo! The days are hast'ning on,
By prophets seen of old,
When with the ever-circling years
Shall come the time foretold,
When peace shall over all the earth
Its ancient splendors fling,
And all the world give back the song
Which now the angels sing.

Skit: "Hark! It's Harold And The Angel Band"

L: As we prepare ourselves once again for the birth of our Savior,
let us make Advent a time of preparation as a community of
faith, not worshiping the angels, but worshiping the God who
made them and created us in his image, the Son who ascended
with the angels and awaits a time to take us to heaven as well,

and the Holy Spirit who directs the angels and us to Jesus. We bind ourselves together now in our confession of faith. Let us rise and declare that faith through the words of the Apostles' Creed.

Apostles' Creed
I believe in God, the Father Almighty,
    Creator of heaven and earth.

I believe in Jesus Christ, his only Son, our Lord.
    He was conceived by the power of the Holy Spirit
        and born of the Virgin Mary.
    He suffererd under Pontius Pilate,
        was crucified, died and was buried.
    He descended into hell.
    On the third day he rose again.
    He ascended into heaven,
        and is seated at the right hand of the Father.
    He will come again to judge the living and the dead.

I believe in the Holy Spirit,
    the holy catholic church,
    the communion of saints,
    the forgiveness of sins,
    the resurrection of the body,
    and the life everlasting. Amen.

Offering

Special Music: "The Little Drummer Boy"

The Angels Take Our Prayers To God

Prayers Of The Church
L: Angels stand before God with their harps and golden bowls full of incense, which are the prayers of the saints. So now we

ask the angels to gather the prayers of this community and to bring them before Jesus. Lord, in your mercy,

C: Hear our prayer.

L: Angels have a ministry toward believers, and so we ask God's Holy Spirit to send the angels to guide us. Lord, send your angels before us and prepare our way. Lord, in your mercy,

C: Hear our prayer.

L: God's angels provided food for Elijah and strength in his journey. Lord, send your angels to care for us. Lord, in your mercy,

C: Hear our prayer.

L: The angel of the Lord encamps around those who fear him and he delivers them. Lord, send your angels to protect us and deliver us from all harm. Lord, in your mercy,

C: Hear our prayer.

L: God's angel came to Paul to encourage him in the face of persecution. Lord, send your angels to comfort and encourage us. Lord, in your mercy,

C: Hear our prayer.

L: As a community in need of your grace, dear Lord, we lift our concerns now before you. (*Community may lift up prayers at this time.*) Lord, in your mercy,

C: Hear our prayer.

L: Lord, your angels have heard our spoken and unspoken prayers. Gather them now with the prayers of all the saints as we lift them to you, trusting in your mercy; through your Son, Jesus Christ, our Lord.

C: Amen.

The Lord's Prayer
Our Father, who art in heaven,
hallowed be thy name,
thy kingdom come,
thy will be done,
on earth as it is in heaven.
Give us this day our daily bread;
and forgive us our trespasses,
as we forgive those
who trespass against us;
and lead us not into temptation,
but deliver us from evil.
For thine is the kingdom, and the power, and the glory,
forever and ever. Amen.

Dismissed With The Angels

Benediction
L: As we have shared in this Advent service, let us be encouraged
and prepared to go forth to be God's angels of love and mercy
to others. Go in the name of the Father, the Son, and the Holy
Spirit. Go in peace. Serve the Lord.

C: Thanks be to God!

Song: "Go Tell It On the Mountain"
Refrain:
Go tell it on the mountain,
Over the hills and ev'rywhere;
Go tell it on the mountain
That Jesus Christ is born!

While shepherds kept their watching
O'er silent flocks by night,
Behold, throughout the heavens
There shone a holy light. (*Refrain*)

The shepherds feared and trembled
When, lo, above the earth
Rang out the angel chorus
That hailed our Savior's birth. (*Refrain*)

Down in a lonely manger
The humble Christ was born;
And God sent us salvation
That blessed Christmas morn. (*Refrain*)

Hark! It's Harold And The Angel Band
An Advent Story

Angel Choir: (*Begin singing offstage and then enter.*)
(**Tune:** Hark! The Herald Angels Sing)
Hark! It's Harold and the Angel Band
Spreading Good News across the land.
Peace on earth to all we bring,
A message clear we're called to sing.
Joyfully we come tonight
To bring glad tidings not of fright.
With our voices raised on high
We sing to Christ a lullaby.
Hark! It's Harold and the Angel Band
Creating God's Christmas once again.

Scene 1: Heaven

(*Street sign with cloud and "Heaven" written on it. Harold and the Angel Choir, dressed in white gowns with haloes, are rehearsing.*)

Harold: Okay, okay ... it's coming. Tenors, you're a little rusty. Haven't you been practicing those carols lately?

Angel 1: My harp needed tuning, so I've been working on that. (*Strums harp.*)

Angel 2: My guitar strings broke, and I needed to wait for a back order. (*Guitar with broken sting is plucked.*)

Harold: And sopranos? Try to reach those high notes without straining. Okay?

Angel 3: My voice is a little tired. I've been telling all the new arrivals about that first Christmas. They're so excited about auditioning for your Bethlehem Concert Year 2000. These new kids on the block weren't part of that first Christmas night, you know. For us oldies but goodies, it seems like only yesterday, but that was almost 2,000 years ago! Wow! How the time flies when you're in the Lord's service.

Harold: Yes, the message stays the same. It's our way of delivery that may have changed. People today aren't into lyres and harps like they use to be, but music in any century is a powerful vehicle for the gospel message.

Angel 1: It sure is. I was just down to earth on my rounds yesterday, and every place I went Christmas music was in the air. This is a great time to be about, stirring people's hearts to be open to receive the Lord Jesus. How blessed human beings are to be God's children, to be temples of God's own Spirit. I'm so envious.

Harold: Okay, remember who you are. That's what got Satan into trouble so long ago. He wanted to be God and was not content to be God's messenger.

Angel 2: Well, I'm happy doing the Lord's bidding. Just look at Gabriel. He really had a great role to take in that first Christmas. By the way, where is he tonight?

Harold: He went to earth on an assignment from God. It seems there are two very lost souls down there who need some direction. Want to join him? We can take a break and go see if he needs any help. The Lord is always seeking the lost, and it makes us so happy when a lost soul returns to the Lord.

Angel 3: Sounds great. But we better not sport our wings. It might scare whoever Gabriel is seeking. Let's put on our street clothes and beam down. Are you ready?

Angel 1: I'm game. Let's go.

Scene 2: Grocery Store

(Turn sign around to read "Heaven's Grocery Store." Table with groceries on it. Paper bags and small carry-out carts nearby.)

Grumpier: Watch out there! You made me drop my "Sweet & Low," Grumpy.

Grumpy: That stuff ain't gonna make you any sweeter, Grumpier. You're so low-down now that nothing added to your life can make it sweeter.

Grumpier: I'm no worse sinner than you. Your disposition ain't much better.

Grumpy: Those are fighting words. Come on, put up those dukes, and let's have at it. *(Drops groceries and puts up fists to fight.)*

Gabe: *(The angel Gabriel, wearing a stock boy's apron, rushes in to break up the fight.)* Come on, Mr. Grumpy. Stop it, Mr. Grumpier. What's the matter with you two? Is that any way for neighbors to treat each other?

Grumpier: And just who are you, you young whippersnapper, to be trying to get us to reconcile our differences?

Gabe: The name's Gabe. I'm a stock boy here and overheard you two collide.

Grumpy: So, how did you know our names?

Gabe: You could say an *angel* told me. I make it my business to know my *boss's* customers. Don't want anyone getting alienated. Mr. Heaven is very concerned about all his people.

Grumpier: Yeah, he just wants our bucks.

66

Grumpy: You spend a lot here, don't you, Grumpier? I see the wad of coupons you have stuck in your sack. Just like Santa Claus openin' his pack! Have to spend $10 at least before you try to cheat Heaven out of your dimes and quarters. I bet you've tried slipping some expired coupons over on the checkout girl. I've seen you flash your sly smile and try to drop some juicy gossip in her ear to distract her.

Grumpier: Put them up! Did you hear that slander, Gabe? He's calling me a cheat, a liar, and a gossip! Now that's assassinating my good character. What are people going to think?

Gabe: Well, is there any truth in the accusation?

Grumpier: Hey! Who died and made you God? He's the only one I'm accountable to.

Gabe: That's right. It's Christmas and a good time to take account of your lives and see where God fits in.

Grumpy: Well, you just report to your boss that we're doing fine just like we are. No need to get things right with each other. We enjoy this sparring.

Background Music: Angel Choir
Hark! It's Harold and the Angel Band
Spreading God's love throughout this land.
Peace on earth and mercy mild,
God wants sinners reconciled.
Joyfully we tell the news
To people in and out of pews
That Jesus Christ was born that day
With his life our ransom paid.
Hark! It's Harold and the Angel Band
Calling all to be born again.

Grumpier: And while you're at it, change that tune on your Muzak. Peace, mercy, joy. Bah, humbug!

Gabe: You don't like the tune? That group happens to be friends of mine. In fact, they're playing a gig right over at your church tonight. Why not come and hear them?

Grumpy: Church? The roof might fall in if Grumpier set foot in there! How long's it been, brother? You stopped going after Ms. Kronke picked me over you to sing "O Holy Night" in seventh grade. Right?

Grumpier: Well, I got to play the drum the next year for "The Little Drummer Boy."

Grumpy: Oh, yeah, I remember now! You beat that thing like an angel flapping its wings!

Gabe: And speaking of angels, I think I hear a band coming now!

Angel Choir: (*Enters wearing street clothes, playing different instruments, and singing*)
(**Tune:** Row, Row, Row, Your Boat)
Flap! Flap! Flap your wings
Angels from on high;
Singing, humming, hear them strumming
Praise to God most high!

Grumpier: What in the world?

Angel 1: No, we're out of this world!

Angel 2: That's right, lost souls. We've come to spread a little Christmas cheer into your dark lives.

Grumpy: *Lost ... dark ...* Hey? Who do you guys think you are calling us *lost* and in the *dark*?

Grumpier: Yeah, and don't lump us together like a blob of humanity. I am not this guy's brother or his keeper.

Angel 3: Well, that's too bad. You have a unique gift we don't have of being soul mates.

Grumpy: Soul mates! That's a chuckle. Me and him brothers? Better take your Christmas cheer down the street. You've got a better chance of singing your song on the highways and byways than here in the grocery store to that Sunday school dropout.

Grumpier: There he goes again! And just why do you think I dropped out of Sunday school, *Mr. Always Had People Who Cared*?

Grumpy: I thought it was 'cause I always got the best part in the Sunday school program, you know, the solo part or Joseph. You just got to hammer on that drum and never could keep a beat.

Grumpier: So much for your insight into my life!

Angel 1: Christmas wasn't always pleasant for you, was it, Mr. Grumpier?

Angel 2: Did anyone ever come to hear you when you had a part?

Grumpier: No. I went all by myself 'cause my folks never had time for that religion stuff.

Angel 3: But you enjoyed your time in church, didn't you?

Grumpier: Yeah! I did.

Grumpy: Then why did you stop coming?

Grumpier: So much for your noticing I was gone! Remember when my grandma got sick and died? She was the one that always made sure I got to church. But when she was gone, there was nobody to drive me there. It was just too far to walk.

Grumpy: Well, why didn't you ask someone to come and get you?

Grumpier: I was so mad that no one even noticed I was missing that I figured you didn't care. So I stopped, and no one ever invited me back. Over all these years I've watched you all get dressed in your Sunday go-to-meeting clothes and never once ask me to come. Not 'til tonight. And it takes an invitation from a stock boy named Gabe and an alternative rock group named...?

Harold: Oh, I'm Harold and these guys are my angel band. Hit it guys!

Angel Choir:
Hark! It's Harold and the Angel Band
Spreading Good News across the land.
Peace on earth to all we bring,
A message clear we're called to sing.
Joyfully we come tonight
To bring glad tidings not of fright.
With our voices raised on high
We sing to Christ a lullaby.
Hark! It's Harold and the Angel Band
Creating God's Christmas once again.

Harold: Now, realize how important you both are to God. He's arranged for a concert right here in the middle of a grocery store to get your attention. Like our second verse goes:

Angel Choir:
Hark! It's Harold and the Angel Band
Spreading God's love throughout this land.
Peace on earth and mercy mild,
God wants sinners reconciled.
Joyfully we tell the news

70

To people in and out of pews
That Jesus Christ was born that day
With his life our ransom paid.
Hark! It's Harold and the Angel Band
Calling all to be born again.

Harold: Yeah, God wants you reconciled ... to him and to each other. Christmas is a great time to begin, for God so loved the world that he came here in the flesh so that all people — grumpy old men and women, lost souls, churchgoers and unchurched folk — all of his children — might have eternal life.

Grumpy: And that is good news! What do you say, brother? Forgive me for not reaching out ... I, well, I just didn't know you had a need. Can I make it up to you by picking you up tonight?

Grumpier: Well, I don't know. It's been so long. Do you think God will still take me back?

Harold: Tell you what! We have it on good authority he will. In fact, it won't cost you a dime! Your way's been paid through the death of his own Son. And tonight, there's no cost. Here's some free tickets to an out of the world concert! Best seats in the house too.

Grumpier: And how will I be received?

Harold: Just as you are.

Grumpy: And you're in luck, you old buzzard. Tonight Dodie Dallipiazza's made the dessert! And she's a great cook! Hey! Why not bring your drum and play a little for us?

Harold: Yeah, you might fit in real well with our backup music.

Grumpier: Okay. Okay. The dessert thing did it. I'll come, but, Grumpy, stick close to me so I don't feel a stranger. All right?

Grumpy: Sure thing. I'll be your keeper ... but just for tonight. There's a few widow ladies there you might want to keep your eye on. Good cooks and real faithful.

Grumpier: Now, now ... no matchmaking. One step at a time. First God, then others, then we'll see where things go.

Harold: Great! We'll see both of you tonight!

Angels: So long, guys.

Harold: Let's have a little traveling music, band.

Angel Choir:
Flap! Flap! Flap your wings
Angels from on high;
Singing, humming, hear us strumming
Praise to God most high!

Ring! Ring! Ring those bells
Angels get their wings;
For each sinner who repents
And makes Jesus Christ their King!

(*Switch tune*)
Hark! It's Harold and the Angel Band
Spreading Good News across the land.

Harold: Good night, all, and a blessed Advent journey. Come and catch our act either on the plains of Bethlehem, your local church, or right here ... for God's in all our business and cares about all of you. Farewell from Harold ...

Angels: And the Angel Band!

(*Group goes out singing*)
Hark! It's Harold and the Angel Band
Announcing Christ throughout the land.
Peace on earth and mercy mild,
We love it when you are reconciled.

(*Switch tune*)
Joy to the world! The Lord has come!
Let earth receive its King!

Angel Choir:
(**Tune:** Hark! The Herald Angels Sing)
Hark! It's Harold and the Angel Band
Spreading Good News across the land.
Peace on earth to all we bring,
A message clear we're called to sing.
Joyfully we come tonight
To bring glad tidings not of fright.
With our voices raised on high
We sing to Christ a lullaby.
Hark! It's Harold and the Angel Band
Creating God's Christmas once again.

Background Music
Hark! It's Harold and the Angel Band
Spreading God's love throughout this land.
Peace on earth and mercy mild,
God wants sinners reconciled.
Joyfully we tell the news
To people in and out of pews
That Jesus Christ was born that day
With his life our ransom paid.
Hark! It's Harold and the Angel Band
Calling all to be born again.

Angel Choir:
(**Tune:** Row, Row, Row Your Boat)
Flap! Flap! Flap your wings
Angels from on high;
Singing, humming, hear them strumming
Praise to God most high!

Hark! It's Harold and the Angel Band
Spreading Good News across the land.
Peace on earth to all we bring,
A message clear we're called to sing.
Joyfully we come tonight
To bring glad tidings not of fright.
With our voices raised on high
We sing to Christ a lullaby.
Hark! It's Harold and the Angel Band
Creating God's Christmas once again.

Hark! It's Harold and the Angel Band
Spreading God's love throughout this land.
Peace on earth and mercy mild,
God wants sinners reconciled.
Joyfully we tell the news
To people in and out of pews
That Jesus Christ was born that day
With his life our ransom paid.
Hark! It's Harold and the Angel Band
Calling all to be born again.

Harold: Let's have a little traveling music, band.

Flap! Flap! Flap your wings
Angels from on high;
Singing, humming, hear us strumming
Praise to God most high!

Ring! Ring! Ring those bells
Angels get their wings;
For each sinner who repents
And makes Jesus Christ their King!

(*Switch tune*)
Hark! It's Harold and the Angel Band
Spreading Good News across the land.

(*Group goes out singing*)
Hark! It's Harold and the Angel Band
Announcing Christ throughout the land.
Peace on earth and mercy mild,
We love it when you are reconciled.

(*Switch tune*)
Joy to the world! The Lord has come!
Let earth receive its King!

Angels In The Outfield

Worship Leader

Songs

"All Day, All Night"
"Hark! The Herald Angels Sing"
"All Hail The Power Of Jesus' Name" (vv. 1, 5)
"Come, Thou Long-Expected Jesus"
"O Little Town Of Bethlehem"
"Take Me Out To The Ball Game"
God's Star-Spangled Banner"
"Oh, Worship The King" (vv. 1, 2, 6)

Three Readers

First Reading: Hebrews 1:1-4 (*The Youth Bible*)

In the past God spoke to our ancestors through the prophets many times and in many different ways. But now in these last days God has spoken to us through his Son. God has chosen his Son to own all things, and through him he made the world. The Son reflects the glory of God and shows exactly what God is like. He holds everything together with his powerful word. When the Son made people clean from their sins, he sat down at the right side of God, the Great One in heaven. The Son became much greater than the angels, and God gave him a name that is much greater than theirs.

Second Reading: Hebrews 1:5-9 (*The Youth Bible*)

This is because God never said to any of the angels, "You are my Son. Today I have become your Father." Nor did God say of any angel, "I will be his Father, and he will be my Son." And when God brings his firstborn Son into the world, he says, "Let all God's angels worship him." This is what God said about the angels: "God makes his angels become like winds. He makes his servants become like flames of fire." But God said this about his Son: "God, your throne will last forever and ever. You will rule your kingdom with fairness. You love right and hate evil, so God has chosen you from among your friends; he has set you apart with much joy."

Third Reading: Hebrews 1:10-14 (*The Youth Bible*)

God also says, "Lord, in the beginning you made the earth, and your hands made the skies. They will be destroyed, but you remain. They will all wear out like clothes. You will fold them like a coat. And like clothes, you will change them. But you never change, and your life will never end. And God never said this to an angel: "Sit by me at my right side until I put your enemies under your control." All the angels are spirits who serve God and are sent to help those who will receive salvation.

Angelic Witness

Angel Witness 1
Angel Witness 2
Angel Witness 3
Angel Witness 4

These four witnesses may dress up as baseball players and carry bats. Find four people to share a story of an angel they know in this world or an angel encounter in their life. Build on each other and insert personal facts in introducing each.

Angels In The Outfield

Opening Song: "All Day, All Night"

Invocation
L: Lord God, we come before you this night asking you to care
for our souls. Send your Holy Spirit down upon us that we
might prepare for the night ahead. We thank you that you have
been with us in the day and will send your angels to watch
over us as we rest. Our souls praise you, King of Heaven. Fill
this place with your heavenly hosts. Fill our souls with praise.
For we call upon you in Jesus' name.
C: Our souls join the angels in praising the King of heaven.

Song: "Hark! The Herald Angels Sing"

L: Tonight we bring our worship as tribute to the King of Heaven.
We praise God for his grace and favor shown to us in Jesus
Christ. God does tenderly shield and spare us. He answers us
when we call out to him. He rescues us from our enemies and
protects us from harm. We have not seen God face to face as
the angels have, but we see him in Jesus and in each other. So
look into the face of your neighbor now and say, "I see Jesus.
I see an angel."

(Congregation greets each other.)

L: Yes, God is present with us tonight and has sent his angels to
be among us. As the sun has set and the moon now rises, we
remember that all the universe bows down praising the God of
Grace. So let us be seated as we prepare our hearts to receive
God's Word as it comes to us in the Holy Scriptures.

First Reading: Hebrews 1:1-4 (*The Youth Bible*)
In the past God spoke to our ancestors through the prophets
many times and in many different ways. But now in these last

days God has spoken to us through his Son. God has chosen his Son to own all things, and through him he made the world. The Son reflects the glory of God and shows exactly what God is like. He holds everything together with his powerful word. When the Son made people clean from their sins, he sat down at the right side of God, the Great One in heaven. The Son became much greater than the angels, and God gave him a name that is much greater than theirs.

Song: "All Hail The Power Of Jesus' Name" (vv. 1, 5)

L: God calls us to worship Jesus with the host of heaven. Hear our second reading.

Second Reading: Hebrews 1:5-9 (*The Youth Bible*)

This is because God never said to any of the angels, "You are my Son. Today I have become your Father." Nor did God say of any angel, "I will be his Father, and he will be my Son." And when God brings his firstborn Son into the world, he says, "Let all God's angels worship him." This is what God said about the angels: "God makes his angels become like winds. He makes his servants become like flames of fire." But God said this about his Son: "God, your throne will last forever and ever. You will rule your kingdom with fairness. You love right and hate evil, so God has chosen you from among your friends; he has set you apart with much joy."

L: The writer of the book of Hebrews here cites verses from the Psalms and 2 Samuel. The Old Testament is filled with messages about God's angels. God's angels worship Jesus, the King, the long-expected King. And so let us worship God's Son, who established his throne on high, with our next song.

Song: "Come, Thou Long-Expected Jesus"

L: Truly Jesus was born to set us free. We bow down with the angels and worship him who was with God from the beginning.

This world will pass away, but our Jesus will never change. And so let us hear our final reading.

Third Reading: Hebrews 1:10-14 (*The Youth Bible*)
God also says, "Lord, in the beginning you made the earth, and your hands made the skies. They will be destroyed, but you remain. They will all wear out like clothes. You will fold them like a coat. And like clothes, you will change them. But you never change, and your life will never end. And God never said this to an angel: "Sit by me at my right side until I put your enemies under your control." All the angels are spirits who serve God and are sent to help those who will receive salvation.

L: Yes, our Lord Jesus is the one God set above the angels and us. And so we praise God for the blessing of salvation and the knowledge that we are set apart to know him as our Savior. Let us praise God with the hosts now as we sing "O Little Town Of Bethlehem."

Song: "O Little Town Of Bethlehem"

L: Yes, we come together with the host of angels and praise God for Jesus Christ. Jesus came to earth and ministered to the many who surrounded him. He gave his life that we might have salvaation, and then left to sit at the Father's right hand. So today, the Holy Spirit ministers to us. And the angels still come to make visits here on earth, sometimes in angelic forms and at other times in the form of humans we encounter. Remember the angels in the movie, *Angels In The Outfield?* They were dispatched in answer to a little boy's prayer. They came with a message of hope and love to a ball game. And so, let us now pray: Creator God, you who made the heavens and earth, who populated both with heavenly beings and humankind, send your ministering angels among us and connect our spirits with yours. In Jesus' name,

C: Amen.

Angelic Witness

Narrator: Hello, I'm Sister Angelica, the Voice of the Angels, coming to you from Angel Park, located right here in your midst. Come along with me as our Lord takes us out to the greatest ball game in town. Let's sing now.

Song: "Take Me Out To The Ball Game"
Take me out to the ball game.
Take me out to the park.
Buy angel food and some crackerjacks,
I don't care if I never get back.
Let me root, root, root for the Angels;
We know they'll win, so we came,
For it's 1, 2, 3 prayers we're in
At the Angels' game.
— words by Sally Karttunen (used with permission)

Narrator: Behold! Angel Park. The teams are ready. The players are prayed up and eager to go. So we begin our game with God's Star-Spangled Banner. Please stand now and sing.

Song: "God's Star-Spangled Banner"
Oh say, can you see
Our Lord Jesus Christ,
Who so proudly we hail
As the Angels come singing?
With bright haloes and wings,
Through the darkness of night,
O'er the houses they watch
As we're gallantly dreaming.
And their robes pure white glare,
Their wings beating the air,
Gave proof through the night
That our Lord's always there.

Oh say, does God's star-spangled banner yet wave;
O'er the souls who have been freed from death and the grave?

> — words by Sally Karttunen (used with permission)

Narrator: Behold the Angel team set before you. We have on the mound the Holy Spirit, who will pitch our first ball to (*Witness 1*), who will share a vision of an earthly angel.

Angel Witness 1: (*Tells personal story.*)

Narrator: And next up to bat is (*Witness 2*).

Angel Witness 2: (*Tells personal story.*)

Narrator: And so, we have (*name*) on second and (*name*) on first. And now up to bat is (*Witness 3*).

Angel Witness 3: (*Tells personal story.*)

Narrator: Well, the bases are loaded. And we need a good hitter, and I see her coming. Who else but that strong woman of prayer who has a strong connection with angels of all sorts as she does battle in prayer and ministers with the best of them? But let's let her bat the team in for a home run. (*Witness 4*), step up to the plate.

Angel Witness 4: (*Tells personal story.*)

Narrator: And it's a home run batting all three bases in. Thanks to all the angels who shared their witness with us tonight and gave us much to ponder about God's ministering spirits. They have told you stories of angels robed in flesh and robed in white. They have told of God's love found in other people and in his Son, Jesus. They have told you of a King whom we all worship and praise. And so let us end our service tonight with our final hymn of praise.

Closing Hymn: "Oh, Worship The King" (vv. 1, 2, 6)

Benediction:

L: Go now in peace. Go and may your night be filled with the presence of God's angels and his Holy Spirit. Go in the name of the Father, the Son, and the Holy Ghost.

C: Thanks be to God. Amen.

A
Christmas
Celebration

A Christmas Celebration
A Candlelight Worship Service For Christmas

Prelude

The Place Of Celebration

Prophecy Announced: Micah 5:2-5a

Song Of Celebration: "O Little Town Of Bethlehem" (vv. 1, 3, 4)

God's People Celebrate

P: The prophet Micah foretold the place of the Savior's birth, the one who would lead his people to celebrate freedom from sin.

C: Lead us to Bethlehem once more as we celebrate the birth of Jesus.

P: Give ear, O Shepherd of Israel, you who lead your people like a flock!

C: Lead us as you led the shepherds to a manger as we celebrate the birth of Jesus.

P: Stir up your might, blessed Holy One, and come and save us!

C: Lead us with your angels to proclaim the Good News as we celebrate the birth of Jesus.

P: Restore us, O God; let your face shine that we may be saved!

C: Lead us by the shining star as we celebrate the birth of Jesus.

P: For a child has been born for us, a son given to us; authority rests upon his shoulders!

C: Wonderful Counselor, Mighty God, Everlasting Father, Prince of Peace, lead us to celebrate Christmas!

Song Of Celebration: "Away In A Manger" (vv.1, 2)

Mary Celebrates

The Gospel Proclaimed: Luke 2:1-7

Special Music Of Celebration

The Angels Celebrate

The Gospel Proclaimed: Luke 2:8-14

Song Of Celebration: "Angels, From The Realms Of Glory" (vv. 1, 2)

The Shepherds Celebrate

The Gospel Proclaimed: Luke 2:15-20

Song Of Celebration: "What Child Is This?" (vv. 1, 2)

Celebration Message: Christmas Homily

Song Of Celebration: "Good Christian Friends, Rejoice" (vv. 1, 2, 3)

A Celebration Of Faith
(Litany based on Philippians 2:6-11)

P: Let us celebrate Christ Jesus, who, though he was in the form of God, did not regard equality with God as something to be exploited.

C: We confess and celebrate God the Father and his Son, Jesus the Christ.

P: Jesus emptied himself, becoming flesh and living among his people.

C: God became the baby Jesus conceived by the Holy Spirit and born of the Virgin Mary.

P: That baby grew, humbling himself, obedient to his Father's will.

C: Our Savior was obedient to the point of death — a death on a cross.

P: Jesus' death and suffering caused God to highly exalt him.

C: Praise to the Savior who died, was buried, descended into hell, and who rose again.

P: God gave him the name that is above every name.

C: We exalt the name of Jesus as we bend our knee with all those in heaven and on earth and under the earth.

P: The ascended Lord, who sits on the right hand of God, will come again to judge the living and the dead,

C: And then every tongue will confess that Jesus Christ is Lord, to the glory of the Father. Amen.

We Celebrate With Our Offerings

Special Musical Offering

Offertory

We Celebrate In Prayer

P: In the beginning was the Word, and the Word was with God, and the Word was God.

C: Praise to the Word who became flesh in the Child of Bethlehem and lived among us.

P: Jesus was in the world, yet the world did not know him.

C: Light of the world, forgive us for not recognizing you in our midst.

P: But to all who received him, who believed in his name, he gave the power to become children of God.

C: Be born anew in us this night, most Holy Child, we pray.

P: As the angels declared the glory of God, fill our mouths with your praise.

C: Glory to God in the highest heaven, and on earth peace among those whom God favors.

P: The shepherds watching their flocks that night were alert to the needs of those in their care.

C: Beloved servant of God, open our eyes that we may see and respond to those you call us to love in your name.

P: Sent forth to behold the Christ Child, the shepherds became the first to witness the Good News.

C: Pour forth your Spirit, Almighty God, empowering us to proclaim Jesus as Lord. Hail the newborn King! The one who lives forever! King of kings! Lord of lords! Amen.

The Celebration Of Holy Communion

Words Of Institution And Distribution

The Lord's Prayer

Communion Carols

Communion Prayer
P: As the shepherds beheld the child in the manger, we behold the man on the Cross. His body and blood, given and shed for our sins, strengthen you in your journey of faith. Go forth into the night wrapped in God's love, singing his praises.

C: The light shines in the darkness as we celebrate the birth of our Savior. Amen.

A Celebration Of Light

Candle Lighting Service

(Torchbearers will light candles of those on end of pews as we sing "Silent Night.")

Song Of Celebration: "Silent Night"

Benediction
P: God has visited his people once again. Go forth and spread the news of salvation to all people declaring your joy to the world. In the name of the Father who loves us, the Son who redeems us, and the Spirit who gives us new life.

C: We declare our joy to the world and truly celebrate Christmas. Amen.

Song Of Celebration: "Joy To The World"